THE TUNNEL

Contents

By
Scot Gardner

Illustrated by
Dean Proudfoot

MW00574817

Frankenbike

Boredom is the mother of insane stunts, something I know for a fact.

It was a gray day one summer, and we were at Meat's place, and we made a Frankenbike from the scrap parts lying behind the shed. Nobody said, "Hey, let's make a bike!" It just happened. Well, Meat and I assembled the bike while Nick watched from a safe distance, dressed as he was in white sneakers.

The monster contraption we made had a standard mountain bike wheel on the back and a plastic scooter wheel on the front, wedged into a pair of racing bike forks that we had to massage with an old axe so they'd fit. It had high-riser handlebars and a bell from a pink bike that Meat said his sister didn't use anymore.

"Dude, lose the bell," Nick suggested.

Meat shook his head and said, "The bell's there to let other people know I have no brakes."

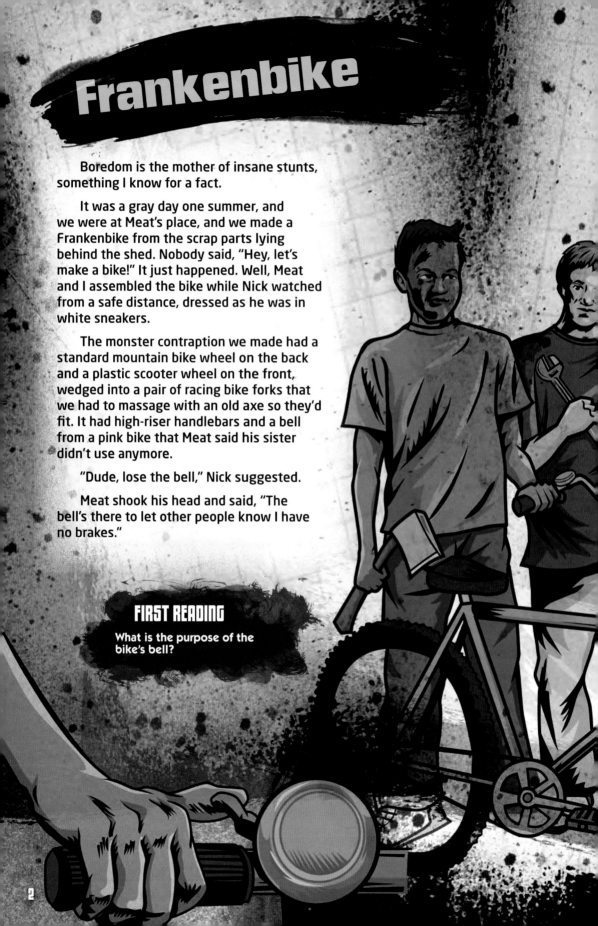

FIRST READING

What is the purpose of the bike's bell?

I laughed. Nick called him an idiot—or words to that effect—and Meat climbed on the beast. The little wheel in front pitched the frame forward, like he was about to fall on his face, and he locked his elbows and made phat motorbike noises with his mouth.

He scootered down the drive, wobbling like a three-year-old without training wheels for the first time, hacked a U-turn, and pedaled to the shed.

"Needs a tune-up," Meat said. "Other than that, it's awesome."

"You need to take it for a spin," Nick suggested. "I'll take videos, and we can post them online! We need to give it a name. Think of a name, Alex."

I looked it up and down and decided it did need a name. We had given life to that wild metal child, so we had to name it. The frame had a sticker on the side that used to say All Terrain, but some of the letters had flaked off. With a bit of help, it was a short jump to the perfect name: *All Terra.*

CLOSE READING

To which literary figure is the title of this section referring? How effective is this title in describing the boys' creation?

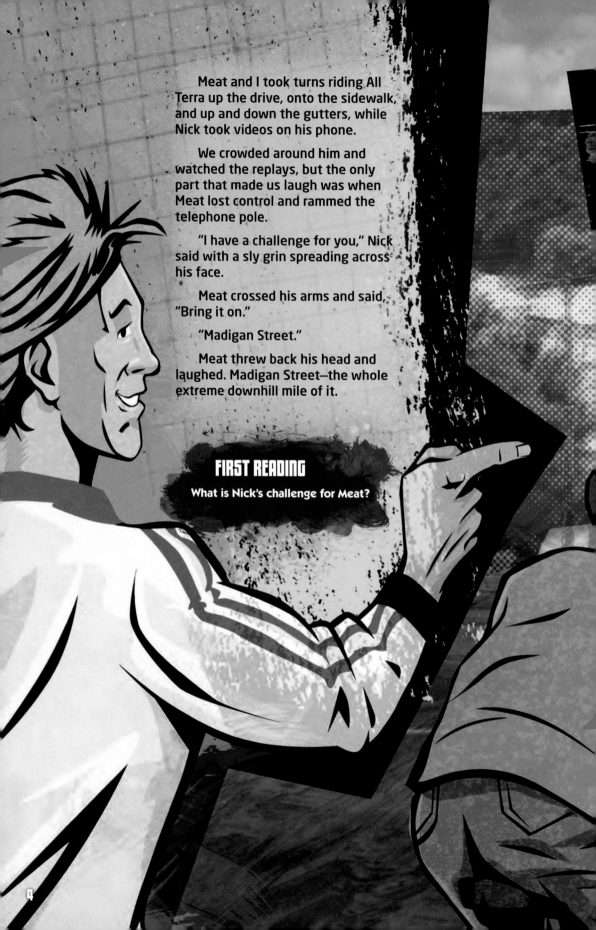

Meat and I took turns riding All Terra up the drive, onto the sidewalk, and up and down the gutters, while Nick took videos on his phone.

We crowded around him and watched the replays, but the only part that made us laugh was when Meat lost control and rammed the telephone pole.

"I have a challenge for you," Nick said with a sly grin spreading across his face.

Meat crossed his arms and said, "Bring it on."

"Madigan Street."

Meat threw back his head and laughed. Madigan Street—the whole extreme downhill mile of it.

FIRST READING

What is Nick's challenge for Meat?

CLOSE READING

What do you know about Nick so far? Using details from the text, create a character description for him.

Stunt

"You're insane," I whispered.

Meat chuckled, "I know that."

He was on the sidewalk, perched on the very top of the hill. Madigan Street fell away below him, empty of traffic except for Nick, who was jogging his way to the bottom. Madigan Street has a reputation.

Tamara Kennedy spent a whole lunch period telling me stories about her street. She said it killed trucks— gave them heart attacks as they hauled their loads up its sheer face. She said if a car hit the bottom of the hill fast enough, it would scrape on the road and sparks would fly. I've seen the deep grooves in the tar way down there, so I believe her stories.

Nick waved and held his phone in front of him.

Meat looked pale, though I could hear him breathing.

"You don't have to do this," I said.

"I know that. I'll be fine."

"Why don't you start halfway down?"

He frowned and said, "If I'm going to do it, it's going to be memorable. I'll either make it and have the video to prove it, or I won't make it, and I'll have the video and the scars to prove that."

Nick was yelling, "Come on! My phone memory is nearly full!"

Meat took a breath, kicked off, and raced away. "Whoooooooohoooooo!"

FIRST READING

What happens if a car hits the bottom of the hill too fast?

He launched off a gutter and took a line down the center of the road. I watched him, then I started to run.

All Terra seemed stable and under control for the first half of the hill. It looked like Meat was at maximum velocity when the speed wobbles hit. His legs shot out for balance, but the wobbles only got worse. He stomped his feet onto the road, and the soles of his sneakers screamed, but the bike didn't seem to slow. The wobbles eased, but Meat kept his shoes hard on the tar.

I know about friction. You can only use your feet as brakes for a certain amount of time until . . .

Meat cried out and lifted his feet just as a black sports car crested the hill behind Nick, engine gunning. Meat swerved, lost control, hit the gutter, and somehow made it back onto the sidewalk. If I hadn't seen the video of Meat's ride a hundred times, I wouldn't have believed it was possible!

He wasn't on the sidewalk for long. Two zigs and one zag later, All Terra's front wheel hit the metal barrier that stopped cars from driving into the creek at the bottom of the hill. It was like someone had pressed the ejector seat button. Meat was catapulted over the handlebars and over the rail—a rolling tangle of limbs, crashing through branches and disappearing from sight.

CLOSE READING

What key details would help you describe Meat's trip down Madigan Street?

Tunnel

The car roared past, oblivious.

Nick was still filming—though he was also smiling and calling out to Meat—when I finally made it to the crashed bike.

As the car crested the hill and the noise of its engine faded, I heard laughter from below.

"Meat?" More laughter. "You OK?"

"Yep," he said. "Whoooooohooooo!"

Nick and I looked at each other and exhaled sighs of relief.

"Hope you got that on the phone," Meat called up. "That was classic!"

"Got it," Nick said. "Come up and check it out."

"The only moving I'm doing for the next ten minutes is shaking," said Meat.

I stepped over the rail. "Come on," I called to Nick.

"I'm not going down there," Nick said. He grabbed the front of his white jacket and frowned at me.

"Don't be that way," I growled.

I picked my way down to where Meat sat on a patch of grass. He was smiling and shaking his head.

"Sure you're OK?"

"Fine," he said. "Check this out."

He pointed to where the creek flowed under the road. There wasn't a bridge as such, just a pipe as tall as me.

CLOSE READING

What detail words does the author use to develop the scene around the tunnel?

"Whooooohoooo!" Meat yelled, and it echoed down the pipe. It went on forever. A semi-fossilized shopping cart lay on its side in the tunnel's open mouth, its ribs covered in potato chip bags and burger wrappers. A rank dribble of rusty water leaked from the base of the pipe. The concrete around the entrance was covered in graffiti tags, most of them featuring the name *Casper* over and over again, but there were some stick figures and a lopsided picture of a skull.

"Looks like All Terra survived," Nick shouted from up on the road. "Little buckle in the front wheel, but other than that, it's fine."

"Bring it down," Meat yelled back.

Silence.

"He doesn't want to get dirty," I said.

"Don't worry about your clothes," Meat yelled. "Come down. We've found a tunnel."

"I've seen the tunnel."

"Have you seen inside the tunnel?"

"It just goes under the road."

Meat was on his feet now so we stepped past the shopping cart and into the throat of the pipe.

Into
the Dark

Ten feet in, it became obvious that the pipe went further than the other side of the road. The darkness and echoey silence came out to greet us. It rode on a cool, damp breeze that smelled faintly of rotting trash. I don't mind admitting that my heart was banging hard. If Meat hadn't been there, I would have bolted back into the light.

Meat strode on confidently for another five steps then stopped and shouted, which made me jump.

There was a loud metal-on-metal crash as something collided with the shopping cart back at the tunnel entrance. It made me cover my ears.

"Here's your bike," Nick shouted. He was a silhouette at the entrance, busily wiping something off his precious jacket.

He walked to where Meat and I were frozen on the edge of the dark and started beatboxing with the echo. Nick is not the best beatboxer on the planet, but it did sound wicked in the tunnel. Meat started grooving, slapping the roof above his head and walking deeper into the abyss. I could see the reflectors on his sneakers, and then he was gone, swallowed by the blackness.

"Meat?"

Nick stopped the beatboxer act, and eventually Meat's voice came back to us: "Come on. Grab the bike. We've got to check this out."

"We haven't got a flashlight," Nick said. "We need a flashlight. Come on, let's go. I have to get changed. We can bring a flashlight back. The bike will be OK there. Nobody will steal it."

swallowed
by the blackness

FIRST READING

What do the boys intend to use for light as they explore the tunnel?

"I'm not worried about it being stolen," Meat said, coming back far enough for us to see him. "I want to ride it."

"In the dark?" Nick asked.

"We can use your phone for light," I suggested.

"Yes!" Meat said. "Let's do this. Let's see where it goes!"

"It stinks in here," Nick said. He took a can of deodorant from his jacket and sprayed the tunnel. "I've got one of those headlamp things at home. It's pretty bright."

"Why are you trying to back out? You won't get dirty in here," I said. "It's all concrete and stuff."

I jogged back to the entrance and untangled All Terra from the cart where Nick had dumped it. I wheeled it back to Meat, and he patted the seat.

"Good beast," he said. "No bucking me off in here, or this tunnel will be your grave."

I held the frame as he climbed on.

"Phone," Meat demanded.

Nick breathed an exasperated sigh and handed Meat his phone. "If you bust it, you owe me five-hundred bucks, OK?"

"Whatever," Meat said.

CLOSE READING

Is Meat a brave or cowardly character? What details from the story this far make you think so?

Nick Goes Down

The feeble light from the screen didn't exactly fill the tunnel, but my eyes adjusted. Meat rode through the thin track of water running along the bottom. Nick and I wide-legged it to straddle the creek and stumble-jogged along to keep up. My heart was still doing its own beatbox thing, but I had a smile on my face. This was the sort of thing summers were meant for. We were in the middle of an adventure.

The tunnel curved gently to the right, and within a minute, the glow from the entrance disappeared and the phone was all we had.

Nick slipped. I heard the dull thud of arms hitting concrete and a tiny splash. He cried out, and I laughed, although I couldn't see a thing. I knew what had happened. "You OK?"

He grumbled under his breath, louder this time, and Meat stopped, asking, "What?"

"Nick fell," I said.

Meat backed the bike up and shone the phone on Nick. His white sneakers now had a greenish-brown stain. He wiped at the slimy mess, but he only managed to spread it further. Meat chuckled.

"Give me my phone," Nick grumbled.

"Why?" Meat asked.

"Just give it to me," he shouted. "I'm going home."

"Come on," Meat said. "We're not to the end yet."

"Do you know how much these shoes cost?" Nick bellowed. "Three hundred bucks!"

FIRST READING

What happens to Nick's sneakers?

CLOSE READING

What examples from your own experience are similar to the peer pressure Meat puts on his friends?

"Yeah well, they're dirty now," I said. "Going home's not going to make them any cleaner."

"True," Meat agreed. "Might as well come along with us and see where this tunnel goes."

"You guys owe me a new pair of pants, too."

"Riiiiight," Meat said. "Whatever you say."

"It's only drain slime," I said. "It'll wash off."

"Phone!" Nick demanded.

"Come on, Nick. Don't get mad."

"Look!" I interrupted. With the phone directed at Nick, the tunnel ahead glowed with a light of its own. "We're nearly there."

the glow from the entrance disappeared

Dead Things

Meat gave Nick his phone and started pedaling toward the glow. I couldn't see a thing on the ground in front of me, but I jogged behind Meat and All Terra, each step a little leap of faith. The light had traveled a long way—I jogged for about twenty miles before we found the source, but it wasn't the end of the tunnel.

The pipe opened into a chamber illuminated from above by the grating in a roadside drain. Roots hung from the ceiling like stalactites. The floor of the room was covered in crushed cans and plastic bottles. A metal ladder was bolted against the wall below the grating. It was good to see the light of day, even though it was 12 feet over our heads.

"Oh, man, what stinks?" Nick said. He'd followed us anyway.

"Wasn't me," I said, but I smelled it, too— the stench of something foul, only this time it was right in my nostrils.

Meat was off the bike and toeing at a hairy ball of something below the drain grating. "Here," he said. "I think it's a cat."

Nick gagged. He whipped his can of deodorant out and gave the cat carcass a good spray. Now the room stank of dead cat and deodorant.

"How do we get out?" Nick asked.

FIRST READING

What are the boys looking for at
the beginning of the passage?

but I smelled it, too—
the stench of
something foul

CLOSE READING

Where in the text does the author
use humor to lighten the mood?
What effect does this have on the
overall tone of the passage?

Meat climbed the ladder and pushed at the manhole cover above his head. It didn't budge. "Not that way."

"Even if we could lift it, we couldn't get All Terra out," I said.

"Then we go out the way we came," Nick said.

Meat dropped down. "We could. That's always an option, but we're not at the end of the tunnel yet. Now stop being a baby. Let's keep going!"

He climbed onto All Terra and pointed it in the direction of the unexplored tunnel. He looked at Nick: "Coming?"

Nick's shoulders drooped, and he turned to face the tunnel we'd come through.

"You can hold the phone," Meat said. "You can also lead the way."

"Why? So any crocodiles in the sewer get me first?"

Meat smiled. "That's the general idea."

Nick called him an idiot—or words to that effect—then he crunched over the trash and into the new tunnel. Meat and I triumphantly bumped fists behind his back.

It wasn't over yet.

FIRST READING

Why does Meat want Nick to go first?

Treasure

Chambers, drains, and trash became more common as we ventured deeper into the pipe. Seeing the daylight every couple of hundred feet made the darkness between seem less threatening. Each new pile of garbage offered treasures as well as disgusting stuff. I made quite a collection of tennis balls. Meat climbed ladders and tested the manholes, but they were all too heavy. He peered out the gutter gratings and relayed what he could see.

"We're in Barkley Street!" he yelled. "I can see the mailbox next door to my dad's office. We're nearly home!"

In reality, however, we were a long way from his home. Unless we found a way out ahead, we'd have to backtrack to where the adventure started—all the way back to Madigan Street.

At the next chamber, the pipe changed. The tunnel leading out was smaller than the one we'd arrived through. The idea of having to bend down while we walked made my guts tighten.

FIRST READING

What happens to the pipe as the boys continue forward?

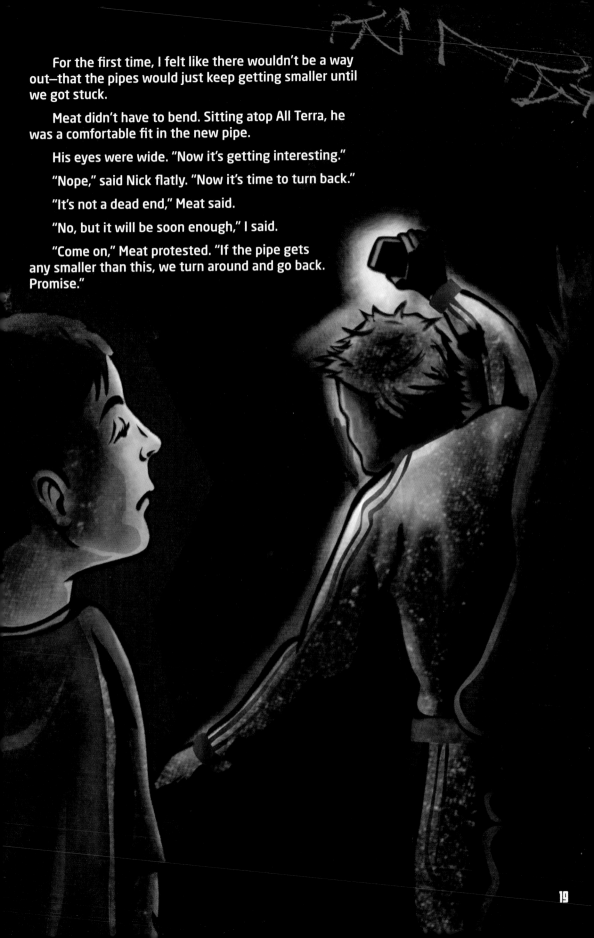

For the first time, I felt like there wouldn't be a way out—that the pipes would just keep getting smaller until we got stuck.

Meat didn't have to bend. Sitting atop All Terra, he was a comfortable fit in the new pipe.

His eyes were wide. "Now it's getting interesting."

"Nope," said Nick flatly. "Now it's time to turn back."

"It's not a dead end," Meat said.

"No, but it will be soon enough," I said.

"Come on," Meat protested. "If the pipe gets any smaller than this, we turn around and go back. Promise."

Nick took the lead again, and I walked right behind him—so close that I kicked him in the heel. Twice.

"Ow! Watch where you're going, Alex."

"Sorry."

"What's the matter with you? Give me some room."

What was the matter with me? The fun was gone. Suddenly, the adventure wasn't an adventure anymore. You take the fun away and it turns into a sort of punishment, a torture. Meat had seemed like the big brave explorer until the fun disappeared. Now he looked like an idiot bossing us around and bent on self-destruction. I didn't want to be part of it anymore. I was ready for it to be over, but I knew it would take almost as long to get out as it had to get in.

I laughed when we burst into another chamber, and the light from the drain above revealed three small pipes. They were just big enough to crawl through, but they stuck out at shoulder height. This was the end. I knew we'd have to turn around. I found another tennis ball and a cigarette lighter that sparked pretty well. I didn't want to waste it, though, so I stuffed it in my bulging pocket.

CLOSE READING

Reread paragraph 5 above. How has the tone of the adventure changed from before? How is this reflected in the text?

"Jackpot!" Nick hollered. "Check it out!"

He'd found a leather wallet. It was misshapen, as if it had been wet and then dried, but when he unzipped it we all sucked in our breath.

It was stuffed with cash: 265 dollars to be exact. There were credit cards, store receipts, and a driver's license.

"Gail Edwards," Nick read. "She lives on Claremont Drive. Don't know her."

"Let me see," Meat said. He took the license and studied the picture, then shook his head. He handed it back to me.

"She looks a little like that girl who works in the video store."

"A little," Nick agreed, and his phone beeped.

"Message?" Meat asked.

I heard Nick swallow. "Low battery."

"You're joking," I said.

He shook his head solemnly.

In the brief silence that followed, we heard music. At least, it sounded like music—faint and buried in white noise, as if the radio wasn't quite tuned in. We had time to look at each other, puzzled, before the small pipe above Nick spewed water onto his jacket.

An Instant River

"What in the world?"

"Somebody flushed the toilet," Meat said with a nasty chuckle.

The two other pipes and the drain above us began dripping.

"It's not the sewer," I said. "It's storm water. This is a storm drain!"

Meat cried out, grabbed All Terra, and shoved it back in the direction we'd come from.

I shoved Nick after him. "Go!" I screamed.

"What?"

"It's raining!"

FIRST READING

What kind of tunnel have the boys found themselves in?

CLOSE READING

Summarize what you know about the characters, using evidence from the text and the inferences you have made.

Evidence from the Text

Inferential Information

Nick   Meat   Alex

Nick's phone beeped like a dying bird. If it died, we'd be in total darkness. The trickle of water beneath our feet had become a flow. We burst into the chamber where the pipe changed size and were instantly soaked by the waterfall that surged in off the road above. We ran, the current ankle-deep and rising.

When the battery in Nick's phone finally gave out, the darkness that swallowed us was complete.

"Noooooo!" Nick howled. His voice echoed along the tunnel and was eventually drowned by the sound of rushing water.

Meat had stopped. "It's OK, Nick," he said. His voice was as reassuring as my mom's in the black of a nightmare. "We can do this. We'll be OK. We just follow the water. One step at a time. Let's go."

However, the darkness was so total that we became disoriented after two or three steps. Nick was whimpering in front of me, and Meat was breathing hard behind me. Trash floating in the water bumped my calves, and I thought I felt the dead cat brush past me. I screamed before I could stop myself.

"There's got to be another tunnel around here somewhere!" Meat yelled. "We just can't see it because it's pitch black." He led us onward, feeling his way with his hand against the concrete wall.

"Even if there is another tunnel out," Nick moaned, "we're going to miss it in the dark."

That's when inspiration struck! I fished the cigarette lighter from my pocket and sparked it. It lit up the tunnel.

"Whoa!" Meat shouted. "Do it again. Again! Alex, you're a genius."

I gave the lighter to Meat, and he used it to crack holes in the darkness between the chambers. We were on the long last leg of the tunnel, with the water pushing at my thighs, when I saw it.

"There!" I cried. "That tunnel to the left. I can see light!"

With the light from the lighter, we found our way into the escape tunnel, and before long, I could see daylight! The rain had never felt so good on my face.

FIRST READING

What events lead up to Nick screaming in the fifth paragraph?

The Legend Lives On

Nick placed the wallet on the counter at the video store. "Recognize this?" he asked the girl working the register. Her nametag said *Gail*.

"Oh my goodness!" she squealed.

She said it must have fallen out of her car. Three days it had been missing, and she was starting to panic. She gave Nick a hundred bucks. What was more surprising was that he gave Meat and I each a cut: $33.35 each. Just when you think you know somebody, they go and mess with your head by being generous!

What about All Terra? The legend lives on. The old beast rests beside the pile of bike skeletons at Meat's place. Nick posted his video of Meat's ride down Madigan Street. Look it up online and prepare to be amazed. That was one insane stunt.

CLOSE READING

How effective is the title of this section as the final chapter of the story?

THINK ABOUT
THE TEXT

MAKING CONNECTIONS

Which of the following connections can you make to the

characters, plot, setting, and themes of *The Tunnel*?

Overcoming a difficult situation   Being scared   Feeling helpless

                                                                                                Making stupid decisions

Experiencing
peer pressure   **TEXT TO SELF**   Experiencing close
                                                                                                friendships
Using your initiative

                                                                                                Dealing with emotions

Doing the right thing

                                                        Making discoveries

                        Facing adversity

TEXT TO TEXT/MEDIA

Talk about texts/media you have read, listened to, or seen that have similar themes. Compare the treatment of theme and the differing author styles.

TEXT TO WORLD

Talk about situations in the world that connect to elements in the story.

PLANNING A CONTEMPORARY FICTION STORY

Contemporary fiction incorporates many different genres, such as mystery, science fiction, adventure, narrative . . .

1 Think about what defines contemporary fiction

Contemporary fiction connects the reader with the complex situations and events of contemporary society. It incorporates themes and contexts that are seen as:

- a reflection of the past
- a mirror of the present
- an indicator of the future

2 Think about the plot

Decide on a plot that has an introduction, problems, and a solution. Write events in the order that they occur.

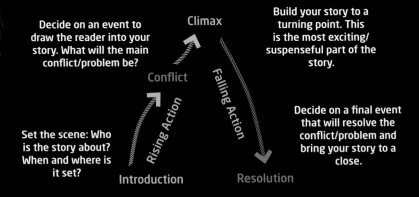

Decide on an event to draw the reader into your story. What will the main conflict/problem be?

Climax

Build your story to a turning point. This is the most exciting/suspenseful part of the story.

Conflict

Falling Action

Rising Action

Decide on a final event that will resolve the conflict/problem and bring your story to a close.

Set the scene: Who is the story about? When and where is it set?

Introduction

Resolution

Think about the sequence of events and how to present it using contemporary fiction devices, such as flashback and foreshadowing.

Flashback = showing part of the story line out of sequence
Foreshadowing = suggesting or indicating events before they happen

3 Think about the characters

Explore:
- how they think, feel, and act
- what motivates their behavior
- their inner feelings, using contemporary fiction approaches, such as stream of consciousness and product-of-society typecasting.

Stream of consciousness = a description of the flow of thoughts and feelings through a character's mind as they arise

Product-of-society typecasting = giving the characters roles that are typical of the society they were born into

4 Decide on the setting

location

atmosphere/mood   time

Note: Contemporary fiction provides a window into current lifestyles and living conditions, which are often shaped by multimedia influences.

WRITING A
CONTEMPORARY FICTION

Have you . . .

- made links to the society and events of your period?

- identified with recurrent contemporary themes?

- maintained a fast pace of action?

- grabbed the readers' attention and dragged them from the first page to the final page?

- been true to the context of your time frame?

- provided a window to the past or present or future?

- explored contemporary values and beliefs?

- developed characters that will stand up to in-depth analysis?

Don't forget to revisit your writing. Do you need to change, add, or delete anything to improve your story?